Thoroughbred

Thoroughbred

A Celebration of the Breed

Photography by

JOHN DENNY ASHLEY

Written by

BILLY REED

SIMON AND SCHUSTER

New York London Toronto Sydney Tokyo

Sɪᴍᴏɴ ᴀɴᴅ Sᴄʜᴜsᴛᴇʀ
Simon & Schuster Building
Rockefeller Center
1230 Avenue of the Americas
New York, New York 10020

sɪᴍᴏɴ ᴀɴᴅ sᴄʜᴜsᴛᴇʀ and colophon are registered
trademarks of Simon & Schuster Inc.

Designed by Laurie Jewell
Printed in Japan by DAI NIPPON PRINTING CO., LTD.

1   3   5   7   9   10   8   6   4   2

Library of Congress Cataloging-in-Publication Data
Ashley, John Denny.
Thoroughbred: a celebration of the breed/photographs by
John Denny Ashley; text by Billy Reed.
p. cm.
1. Thoroughbred horse.   2. Race horses—United States.   3. Horse-
racing—United States.   4. Thoroughbred horse—Pictorial works.
5. Race horses—United States—Pictorial works.   6. Horse-racing—
United States—Pictorial works.   I. Reed, Billy, date.   II. Title.
SF293.T5A84   1990
636.1'32—dc20   89-48721
CIP
ISBN 0-671-66440-9

ACKNOWLEDGMENTS

Linda, Don, and Johnny Johnson for their encouragement; Michael J. Carpenter for his guidance in the complex world of the thoroughbred industry; Robert Diaz, my assistant, for this book, who always stayed one step ahead of my needs; John Lawrence, Bill Straus, and Tony Leonard for their help and advice; the MINOLTA MPA Program, John Jonny, and Phil Braden, who lent both their personal support and the most advanced equipment available to help make this work such a pleasure; the personnel of Keenland, Saratoga, Churchill Downs, Pimlico, Belmont, Hialeia, Gulfstream, Turfway, River Downs, Triple Crown, and Breeder's Cup; the starting gate crew, trainers, exercise riders, jockeys, and outriders, who face very real dangers daily; the owners, managers, and employees of all thoroughbred breeding farms, whose dedication and care make this industry the most beautiful business in the world; Airdrie Stud, The Alchemy, Ashford Stud, Ashleigh Stud, Ashview, Audubon, Ballindaggin, Beaconsfield, Bedford, Bel-Mar, Belmont, Betz Big Sink, Bluegrass, Bluegrass Heights, Brandyleigh, Brookdale, Brookside, Brownwood, Buckland, Buck Pond, Buckram Oak, Burbon Hills, Bwamazon, Calumet, Castleview Equine, Cave Hill, Cherry Valley, Circle O, Claiborne, Clarkland, Clovelly, Copeland, Creek View, Crescent, Crestfield, Crimson King, Crystal Springs, Darby Dan, Dearborn, Deer Lawn, Dixiana, Domino Stud, Donamire, Eaton, Echo Valley, Elkhorn Place, Elmendorf, Fair Acres, Fell Hollow, Flying I, Forest Retreat, Gainesway, Gainesborough, Glencoe, Glencrest, Glen Echo, Golden Chance, Greentree Stud, Hagyard, Hamburg Place, Hermitage, High Adventure, Highclere, Hill 'n Dale, Hillbrook, Hurricane Hall Stud, Hurstland, Idle Hour, Indian Creek, Jonabell, J. T. Lundy, Juddmonte, Katalpa, King Ranch, Lanark, Lanes End, Loch Lea, Manchester, Mandysland, Mare Haven, Margaux Stud, McCoy, Mereworth, Mill Ridge, Mulholland Brothers, Normandy, Northridge, Nuckols, Oak Tree, Overbrook, Parish Hill, Patchen Wilkes, Payson Stud, Pegasus Stud, Pillar Stud, Pinn Oak, Plum Lane, Ponjola, Runnymead, Saxony, Shadowlawn, Shadwell, Shawnee, Spendthrift, The Stallion Station, Stone, Stonereath, Strodes Creek Stud, Summerwind, Taylor Made, Three Chimneys, Tom Gentry, Van Berg, Vinery, Walmack International, Warnerton, Waterford, Whitney, and Wimbledon and to all those who participated directly and indirectly in the preparation of this book.

Thank you for your faith, caring, and support.

John Denny Ashley

My sincere thanks to Charles Rue Woods and Charles Hayward, for their support and encouragement; to turf writers Jim Bolus, Dan Farley, Dale Austin, and Mike Barry, for their help and friendship; to horsemen D. Wayne Lukas, Woody Stephens, Shug McGaughey, John Veitch, Laz Barrera, Pat Day, Jack Van Berg, Seth and Arthur Hancock, John Sosby, Billy Turner, Ted Bassett, and many others for their time and cooperation; to racing publicists Steve Schwartz, Edgar Allen, Jim Williams, Jane Goldstein, Karl Schmitt, and Joe Tanenbaum, for making the job easier; to Carlene Daugherty, for her help and hard work; to my daughters, Amy and Susan, in the hope they will enjoy racing as much as their dad has; and, finally, to my wife, Donna, for her love and understanding.

Billy Reed

This book is dedicated to
Charles Rue Woods for his faith, vision,
and for turning a beautiful dream
into a reality.

ON THE MORNING OF A CLASSIC RACE, be it the Kentucky Derby or the Breeders' Cup Classic or any of the others that racing people cherish above all, the mood on the backstretch is electric with tension and anticipation. To the outsider, watching a trainer chat quietly with turf writers between sips of coffee from a Styrofoam cup, it may look tranquil, even serene. The quiet is broken by the squealing of birds, the gentle nickering of horses waiting to be fed, the chattering of sleepy-eyed grooms. Yet appearances deceive, and beneath the placid exterior there is the knowledge that, based on what happens that afternoon in the big race, lives and careers and even fortunes will ebb and flow.

So it goes today, so it will go tomorrow. The names and faces may change, but the game remains the same. This sense of permanence, and continuity, is part of racing's enormous charm. It has been said that once you belong to the racetrack, you will never lack for a home. And what ties it all together, for the billionaire owner as well as the lowly groom, is a love for racehorses in general, and in particular for those special horses, the ones that owners and breeders and trainers spend their lives seeking. Only once, if he's lucky, will a horseman be blessed with a thoroughbred swift enough and strong enough to chase the legends in the races that, over the years, have emerged as the classics, the ones coveted by everyone who has ever watched a newborn colt struggle to his feet.

At the track, such an animal isn't often called by name. He is, simply, "the big horse." So on the morning of a classic, as the cynosure of all eyes is led from his barn for his final gallop, a groom is apt to call, "Everybody outta the way. . . . Big hoss comin' out." An exercise boy perched regally on his back, he'll be led slowly to the track, usually followed by his trainer and a gaggle of sleepy-eyed reporters. The trainer looks confident, but his restless eyes betray him. Come the afternoon, he will either taste champagne and take his place in the history books, or else be left to wrestle mentally with the bitterness of opportunity missed and promise unfulfilled.

Of a morning, the racetrack is not a world of champagne and floral wreaths and cheers and television cameras. It is a business place, because the horses who run in the classics are worth millions. The smallest lapse in judgment can result in a tragic error. So no wonder the trainer of a "big horse" strains to see his star out there on the track, coming around the turn and out of the lingering mist, the lesser horses giving way without being asked. Here he comes, hooves pounding, clods of dirt flying. When he pulls up, snorting for breath, and begins the walk back to the barn, there to be covered with a blanket and "cooled out," the trainer scans him with practiced eye, looking for the slightest hint of a limp or a pimple on the glossy coat gleaming in the sun. Seeing nothing, the trainer sighs and leaves the barn area, his work—but not his worries—done.

Like a traveling circus, the pursuit of the classics moves across the country, from the warm climates of Florida and California to the traditional spring and summer venues of Kentucky, Maryland, and New York. And like a theater company, it hides its backstage drama behind a breathtaking show of glitter and glamour. It is a world that reaches back into the triumphs and tragedies of the past even as it reaches out, ever optimistically, to the dramas of the future. When two thoroughbreds are bred, the result can be anything. A yearling sold for $3 million at auction may not win a race, and another bought for $17,500 might win the Kentucky Derby. This is the mystery that hooks people on racing and that makes every day at the track an occasion to toast the goddess of luck.

On the afternoon of a classic, the hours pass quickly in a swirl of color and excitement, no matter whether it's a balmy spring afternoon in Kentucky or a lush August day in Saratoga, New York, or the Hollywood-premiere atmosphere of Santa Anita in California. There might be a line of limousines behind the grandstand, and trailer trucks from this television network or that one, with cables snaking out to where cameras are set up to catch every angle of the race for the fans around the nation. In the exclusive areas of the clubhouse, photographers scramble to get a shot of a movie star or an oil sheik or a famous owner's family. Coats and ties are de rigueur for the men, while the women are adorned with the latest designer fashions from New York or Paris or Beverly Hills. From the jockeys' room to the press box, from the cool, fragrant paddock gardens to the tote boards blinking in the infield, the talk is about the big race and the big horse. Can he do it? Will he be upset?

Amid such speculation, the trainers move smoothly, their wide smiles and firm handshakes belying the butterflies fluttering in their stomachs. In the paddock, a half hour or so before the race, the trainers huddle with the owners and jockeys for last-minute strategy talks. Intent on catching each other's words, they are oblivious to the darting photographers or the milling bystanders. Finally it's time for the trainers to give the riders a leg up on the prancing thoroughbreds, who already are so excited by the crowd and the noise that their grooms have to keep them under an extratight hold until turning over the reins to the riders. Then off they go, in single file, around the saddling ring a final time before heading down the chute that leads from paddock to track. When a fan yells encouragement to the jockey aboard the big horse, he smiles, winks, and waves his whip confidently.

Then, finally, the bell sounds and the gates spring open, moving the throng to stand and gasp and yell and cheer in emotional release. And here they come, these beautiful and courageous warriors, straining against each other and against the stopwatch and against history itself, just as they have been bred to do. At a classic, pulses beat quicker, blood rushes harder, emotions bubble closer to the surface. And no matter if the winner is the big horse or some other, he will take his place in the pantheon of champions, the elite list of the great performers who elevate racing from mere sport to marvelous spectacle.

O N A BRIGHT SPRING DAY, amidst the blue-green splendor of a Kentucky breeding farm, month-old foals frolic together beside their grazing mothers. For these young thoroughbreds, it is a long way from the great racetracks of the world, where their older, powerful cousins thunder and battle amidst the colors and roar of the crowd. Indeed, the odds are that many of these young horses will never make that journey, and of those who do, many will not succeed. But it is a peculiar and enduring part of horse breeding that, for the men and women who raise them, every new foal brings with it a special kind of hope. When farmhands watch a newborn foal struggle to its feet, they cannot help but wonder if this might be the one to grow strong enough, brave and fast enough to win the Kentucky Derby, the Preakness, or Breeders' Cup Classic.

A thoroughbred is a select, extraordinary animal—each horse an inheritor of a bloodline that includes some of the elite horses in racing history. In any given breeding season, the mixing of two such noble bloodlines might just strike that special spark that makes a great racehorse, that will to compete and win that burned within a Man o' War or Seattle Slew. It is for this spark that horse breeders work, plan, and spend enormous amounts of money.

Breeding is the foundation of the horse business. Among the wide green pastures and neatly painted fences and barns of the breeding farm, horse breeders match and mix bloodlines like alchemists. Here, some of horse racing's legendary champions pass on their precious bloodlines; horses such as Secretariat, Spectacular Bid, and Nijinsky II are mated with well-pedigreed mares, even as other mares are delivering sons and daughters of the same stallions.

Thoroughbred breeding is an enormous business, and a worldwide endeavor, but the best stallions and mares are still to be found within a fifty-mile radius of Lexington, Kentucky. Known for its distinctive bluish-hued grass and the extraordinary number of good horses—winners of stakes races—it produces, this region is truly a cradle of champions. Such names as Calumet Farm, Claiborne, Spendthrift, Gaines-way, C. V. Whitney, Darby Dan, Greentree Stud, Three Chimneys, and Hamburg Place—among others —evoke echoes of glorious races, great horses, and not infrequent disappointments. The men and women of these Kentucky farms are at once neighbors, rivals, and allies. Like the horses themselves, the humans who breed, train, and race them share a singular world based on a fiercely competitive spirit.

Thoroughbred breeders generally fall into two categories: those who breed to sell and those who breed to race. On the one hand, commercial breeders are in the business of selling bloodlines: their best efforts are sold off to high-bidders at the world-renowned yearling auctions at Keeneland in Lexington, Kentucky, and Saratoga, New York. Private breeders, on the other hand, raise their horses to race under their own farm's particular colors. Between these two are a smaller, third group: those breeders who choose which of their own horses to keep and which to sell.

Whichever the type of breeder, their goal is to raise horses of speed, stamina, beauty, nobility, and most of all, that mysterious, winning spark. For commercial breeders, the proof of their efforts is in the prices their yearlings bring at auction. Private breeders measure their success on racetracks from Churchill Downs to Santa Anita to such high-stakes European races as the Epsom Derby and the French Prix de l'Arc de Triomphe. All the while, both private and commercial breeders battle fiercely to attract new stallions and mares that have finished their racing careers.

The rights to a bloodline come dear. At Claiborne Farm, at Paris, Kentucky, the total value of the stallions and broodmares is well over $100 million. For great stallions, alliances are formed. Known as syndicates, groups of horse owners band together to mutually control the lifetime breeding rights of a colt, rights that have been sold for as much as a world-record $36 million. Among racing thoroughbreds, nearly all fillies become broodmares, while only the very best colts become stallions. (In Kentucky, the ratio of stallions to mares is about 1 to 15.) But not all successful racing colts make great stallions. Citation, the 1948 Triple Crown winner, never sired a colt or filly that came near his own racing brilliance and was considered a failure as a breeding stallion. At the huge prices horses can command, an unpleasant surprise or a mistake in judgment can cost a breeder dearly. One too many of these can drive a breeder from the business.

To be successful, breeders trace bloodlines back generations and plan as far as three years in advance for viable matings. Breeders know a pantheon of horses dead and alive, and they peer into bloodlines in search of latent strengths and weaknesses, physiological and emotional quirks. In the end, some breeders admit, it hardly rises to the level of a science. Says Warner L. Jones, Jr., of Hermitage Farm, "If I guess right, I'm a genius. If not, I've lost money."

The breeding season generally begins on February 15 and ends about July 1. In most cases, breeders transport their mares to a stallion's farm to be bred—a stallion is bred to around forty mares a year. Often, broodmares are flown to Kentucky from as far away as California and Europe to be bred. On all breeding farms, stallions are kept in private paddocks—to prevent them from fighting with one another. The mating takes place under the carefully controlled supervision of specially trained hands. Usually mares are bred back to stallions about two weeks after giving birth.

A mare's pregnancy lasts about eleven months. Most foals are born in March, April, and May. On a large farm, as many as forty or more foals will be born during the spring. In a typical year, more than 9,000—or 20 percent of the nation's total—may be registered in Kentucky alone.

A human being takes a year to learn to walk, but a foal rises to its feet within hours of being born —in a day it will be able to run on stiff and spindly legs. Mares and their foals are turned out together in paddocks as soon as possible. At two weeks, a foal is wormed and has its feet trimmed. At two months, foals are placed in individual paddocks where they are encouraged to eat their fill of the famed bluegrass, which is rich in mineral content.

No matter what month they were born, under the rules of racing all foals become a year old on the ensuing January 1. Between then and the summer months, yearlings are taught the rudiments of racing. Young horses must be trained to stand and wear a bridle. It is during this time of training that commercial breeders begin to groom their yearlings in preparation for the big summer sales.

The great Kentucky farms are almost mechanically efficient—the hands at a typical farm wear starched khaki uniforms—but the bond that develops between breeders, hands, and baby horses is something quite apart from a business. Breeders and their hands know that the road to racing glory is grueling and often cruel. Triumphs occur at the cost of frequent disappointment even at the most successful farms. And sometimes the greatest hopes are dashed by the very worst downfalls. Consider the history of Claiborne Farm and one of its most glorious colts, Swale.

Founded in 1910, Claiborne was made great in the 1940s by A. B. "Bull" Hancock, a legend among Kentucky horsemen. Hancock was a leader in bringing horses to the United States from England —and boosting American breeding to new heights. Hancock's consuming goal in life was to breed and own a Kentucky Derby winner. But despite all the champions he produced for more than three decades, he died in 1972 without ever seeing Claiborne's bright orange silks carried to victory in the Derby.

The last Claiborne horse to win a stakes race under Bull Hancock was a filly named Tuerta. In 1980, having been retired to the farm as a broodmare, Tuerta was bred to Seattle Slew, the Triple Crown champion of 1977. The following year, in 1981, Tuerta gave birth to a dark bay colt. That spring, the horse momentarily disappeared from the farmhands who watched over his progress. They found him an instant later—hidden by a deep swale in the green farm pasture.

Swale became the first colt to win the Derby for Claiborne Farm in May of 1984. Claiborne president Seth Hancock, the younger of Bull Hancock's two sons, paid homage to his father and his last stakes winner, Tuerta. Five weeks later, Swale galloped to an impressive victory in the Belmont Stakes in New York. Now there could be no doubt, the spark of greatness was burning, and Claiborne looked forward to Swale's career as a breeding stallion. But eight days after the Belmont, in the Belmont Park stable area, Swale suddenly reared, keeled over, and died of what was thought to be a heart ailment. After an autopsy, Swale's remains were returned to Claiborne and buried in a little cemetery reserved for the farm's great horses.

Claiborne fell under a pall. "It was hard for me to look at the faces of the guys who had raised and worked with him," Seth Hancock recalled later.

For weeks the farm was inundated with expressions of sympathy from around the nation— hundreds of letters, telegrams, poems, and flowers poured in. Perhaps this more than anything typifies the way a great horse can touch people who have seen him in movement, in the heat and fury of competition or in the calmer moments away from the track.

"He was worth a lot of money, but he was worth a lot in sentiment, too," Hancock said. "He had a lot of racing in front of him." And in a world of bloodlines, he had a chance to pass on his own unique and fiery essence.

Claiborne had not fully recovered from the blow when, in 1986, hope was reborn in a yearling named Forty Niner. By the time he turned three, Forty Niner became the farm's first legitimate Kentucky Derby contender since Swale, and the whole morale of the farm picked up. Once again, in a young horse, the long path to glory lay revealed.

Such is the passion of the breeding farm. On a crisp, late-winter morning a newborn foal struggles to its feet and takes its first tentative steps. A sparkle comes into the human eyes that watch. The odds say that this horse will never win a stakes race. But the mystery of the blood runs deep, and who is to say that this one will not go all the way?

IN THE SUMMER OF 1943, a major thoroughbred auction was held at Keeneland in Lexington, Kentucky. Kentucky horse breeders were making a break with the past. For the first time in twenty years, they had decided not to ship their yearlings east to Saratoga, New York, where the wealthiest horse buyers and best breeders had gathered every summer throughout the twenties and thirties for an annual auction of prized Kentucky yearlings. In 1943, the bluegrass breeders decided to save time, money, and trouble and have an auction close to home. The year 1943 marked the first annual summer sale at Keeneland.

Today, while yearlings are sold at public auction in most racing states and in Europe on a virtual year-round basis, the best sons and daughters of the best sires in the world are auctioned off at the Keeneland July select sale. Once a year, for two consecutive days, the plush, air-conditioned Keeneland sales pavilion becomes a unique gathering place for an unparalleled array of oil barons, sheiks, tycoons, jet-setters, and Kentucky horsemen—the men in cool summer jackets, the women in chic designer fashions. On the elevated auctioneer's podium, the auctioneer, wearing a tuxedo, calls out an incantation:

"Who'll gimme fiftynow. . . . Who will gimme fiftynow. . . . Wilya gimme fiftynow. . . ."

Among the seats, heads bob imperceptibly. Martinis are sipped. The sales catalogues are reexamined. Tuxedo-clad auctioneer's assistants scramble, politely frisking the audience for the next bid. One nod of the head, and the price jumps. A final nod; a million or more dollars may just have changed hands. In the hallway outside the pavilion, spectators stand on tiptoe with their noses pressed against the window, hoping to catch sight of some of the rich and famous who have come to spend their money for a horse or two.

The objects of all this glamour and excitement are mere children; gangly, wide-eyed year-old horses that have never raced a single race or won a single prize, but whose bloodlines and beauty place them among the most expensive—and risky—investments in the world. One by one, as the auction progresses, these startling creatures are led into a cordoned-off area before the crowd just below the podium, each one identified by a numbered tag on its hip. While the auctioneer chants, and an electronic tote board blinks out the increasing bids, the young, long-legged horse stands gleaming before the crowd.

In the 1943 Keeneland sale, 312 yearlings were sold for an average of $2,979—a highly successful auction. In the 1985 sale, the average price paid was over $400,000, an average bolstered by an extraordinary world record for a single yearling, $13.1 million. While the price of everything has gone up over the years, the price of the world's most beautiful, pedigreed racehorses has exploded beyond anyone's wildest dreams.

Thoroughbreds, money, and high society have always gone hand in hand. At the turn of the century, before they began shipping horses east to the Saratoga summer sales, Kentucky breeders sold their yearlings at their own farms, hosting lavish gatherings set against a backdrop of colonial mansions and rolling green hills, serving strong, cool mint juleps to put the local gentry in the buying mood. Over the years, as the reputation of Kentucky horses and their bloodlines grew, buyers began to come from farther and farther away, until today at the Keeneland July sale, it is not uncommon to glimpse Hollywood and sports celebrities, as well as potentates and businessmen from Saudi Arabia, New Zealand, Japan, Australia, France, and England.

Like the old-fashioned Kentucky sales, no expense is spared to put today's prospective customers in the right frame of mind. The major breeders throw lavish parties featuring entertainment that has included such performers as Bob Hope, Burt Bacharach, and Paul Anka. Anita Madden of Hamburg Place Farm is famed for her Keeneland entertaining; each year she turns a tack room into a salon where customers can sip drinks and watch movies in air-conditioned comfort. With its elegant trappings, its long lines of glistening limousines, and the regal atmosphere of a balmy Kentucky evening, the auction today remains true in essence to its genteel roots.

Long before the first Keeneland select-sale party is planned, however, the important business of choosing horses for inclusion in the catalog is begun. This process starts early in the year, when breeders nominate their best yearlings to a four-man pedigree selection committee. James E. "Ted" Bassett III is Keeneland's board chairman, and he oversees the process. Bassett explains:

"We take each nominee and put its pedigree into a computer. A pedigree history through four dams is printed out. Then the selection committee evaluates the nominees and grades them A, B, or C. An A automatically gets in. Generally, that's the offspring of a stakes-placed producing mare and a commercially attractive stallion. The Bs are marginal and must have outstanding individual conformation to get in. The Cs are eliminated."

Once the grading system is completed, two veterinarians inspect all the As and Bs. Yearlings with obvious physical defects are eliminated, no matter what the pedigree. Of the over one thousand horses nominated every year, only a third are finally deemed worthy for inclusion in the summer catalog.

While the selection process is under way, Keeneland officials are busy accepting and considering requests for the 795 seats in the sales pavilion. Established buyers with excellent credit ratings are preferred. A new buyer can be assured a seat if he or she has impeccable credentials and references.

While great care is taken in assigning each seat in the pavilion to a buyer, it is generally easier to control the quality of the horses than the quality of the patrons. Keeneland officials tell the story of a farmer who entered the bidding for a yearling under the impression that the figures being quoted were in the hundreds of dollars rather than the thousands. He bought a yearling for $66,000, then tried to write a check for $6,600. Embarrassed officials had to put the yearling back in the ring and sell it again.

And then there is the story of one Wendell P. Rosso of Newport News, Virginia, and his 1968 bidding war against the man generally deemed to be the richest in the world at that time, Charles Engelhard.

Engelhard had made his fortune in platinum. Along with his team of American, Irish, and English advisors, he was well-known to Keeneland officials and spectators and had been assigned choice seats near the front of the pavilion. When a filly by Sea-Bird was led into the ring, Engelhard began to bid.

As the bidding progressed, Engelhard found himself in a duel with an unknown man in the rear of the pavilion. The newcomer was, as it turned out, the owner of a supermarket chain, but he had no assigned seat and had not bothered to put on a coat or tie. As the bidding escalated, Keeneland officials began to squirm.

"Every time Engelhard made a bid, he was countered from the back by Rosso," Ted Bassett recollects. "When it reached $300,000, Engelhard's advisors told him to drop out, but he kept going. He finally bid $400,000, which was then a world record, and the pavilion erupted. But as soon as the noise died down, Rosso bid $405,000. Engelhard stopped. Then the place really buzzed."

Apprehensively, Bassett approached Rosso.

"Have you established your credit?" asked Bassett.

Coolly, Rosso pulled out four $100,000 certified checks and said, "Is that sufficient?"

As a postscript to the story, it should be noted that the $405,000 filly went on to an entirely undistinguished career.

As soon as a horse is sold, a Keeneland functionary hustles to the buyer's seat to get his signature on a sales slip. If a yearling brings a record, or if the bidding has been particularly spirited, the audience often falls into applause and whistling, until both the breeder and the buyer stand to take a bow.

It takes a sharp eye to see who is bidding during the auction. A bid of $100,000 can be as subtle as a slight movement of the head. The auctioneer and his bid takers are as alert as hawks. As independent contractors working on a commission, it is their job to push the bidding as aggressively as they can.

Frequently, buyers remain anonymous—hiring agents to act on their behalf. If word gets out that a noted trainer is interested in a particular yearling, the price of the horse is sure to climb, and bidding can become savage.

One trainer who often buys through agents is D. Wayne Lukas. In the 1980s, Lukas teamed up with former pro football owner Eugene Klein of San Diego. Since 1983 the combination of Lukas's shrewd horse judgment and Klein's bankroll has proved a winning one. Between 1983 and 1988, Klein spent almost $39 million at public auction. His return was more than three hundred victories, more than $19 million in purses, nine Eclipse Awards for championships, a Kentucky Derby, a Preakness, and seven Breeders' Cup trophies. Working with Lukas, Klein was the owner of both Lady's Secret, the 1986 Horse of the Year and all-time female earnings champion, and Winning Colors, who became only the third filly ever to win the Kentucky Derby.

For such professional horsemen as D. Wayne Lukas, the Keeneland sale is a time for total concentration, savvy, and not a few prayers. Along with other buyers, Lukas spends days ahead of time examining the yearlings, checking their conformation—their individual physique—and pedigree. Lukas himself bases so much of his judgment on how a horse looks that he doesn't examine a horse's pedigree until after he has gone through his personal grading system on conformation alone. Lukas explains, "If I know a horse is a full brother to this champion or that one, I might be inclined to see things that aren't there." To find a yearling's pedigree, a prospective buyer need only look up the hip number in the sales catalogue.

Buying a thoroughbred at auction has always been a financial risk. But in today's market the risk is greater than ever. Many Kentucky horse people trace today's era of fantastic prices back to a single horse, Northern Dancer.

Bred at Windfields Farm, Northern Dancer was sired by Nearctic. In 1964, the little bay colt went on to win both the Kentucky Derby and the Preakness before being retired to stud at Windfields Farm.

Because of his offspring's success in Europe, the Northern Dancer bloodline became highly coveted by foreign buyers, and in particular by a syndicate of oil sheiks led by Mohammed bin Rashid al Maktoum of the United Arab Emirates nation of Dubai, and an English syndicate headed by soccer-pools baron Robert Sangster.

Throughout the 1970s, bidding wars broke out between the two syndicates. During that time, the million-dollar barrier for a yearling fell, and the record escalated quickly to $1.7 million in 1980, $3.5 million in 1981, and $4.25 million in 1982. Then came the quantum leap to the incredible $10.2 million paid in 1983 for a son of Northern Dancer bred by Don Johnson, a former coal-mine operator from eastern Kentucky. Johnson predicted that "this record will sit there a while." He was wrong. Two years later Sangster paid $13.1 million for a son of Nijinsky II (himself a son of Northern Dancer), bred by Warner L. Jones, Jr., William S. Farish, and William S. Kilroy.

Why does someone pay $13 million dollars for an untried, unproven yearling? The answer is as complex as the world of horse racing itself. There is the gamble that the horse will pay off at the racetrack and the stud farm. There is the pleasure and pride of owning a truly beautiful, intricately bred animal— the equine equivalent of a painting by Rembrandt or Van Gogh. There is the prestige of winning in a competition against other wealthy men and women. Horse racing is all of these things: beauty, competition, pleasure, profit, pride, and risk.

Risk most of all. For its $13.1 million, the Sangster syndicate got a horse named Seattle Dancer, who ran in Europe, never won any major stakes races, and was returned to Kentucky for stud duty.

On the other side of the coin is the story of the yearling Wajima, sold at Keeneland in 1973 for a then-record $600,000. Wajima became such a fine runner that he was syndicated for $7.2 million. Or the case of a little-known trainer from Maryland named Grover G. "Bud" Delp, who came to a lesser Kentucky auction with his main client, a Baltimore businessman, Harry Meyerhoff, and walked off with a spotted gray colt for $37,000. Having prepared themselves to bid as high as $60,000, Delp and Meyerhoff laughed afterward that they were already $23,000 ahead. Remembers Delp, "Harry turned and handed the slip to me, as he always does, and said, 'Here's your champion.' We laughed and went back to the barn for a drink."

The horse turned out to be Spectacular Bid, winner of the Kentucky Derby, 1980 Horse of the Year, and a runner of such brilliance that Meyerhoff was able to syndicate him for $22 million in 1980.

For men who make their living preparing thoroughbreds for the grinding challenge of the racetrack, there is, with every great horse, a moment of recognition. Sometimes this moment comes on a quiet morning on the home farm, watching a yearling gambol alone on an expanse of rolling green pasture. Sometimes it happens at a training track, while a two-year-old makes one of his first runs. The trainer suddenly looks down at his stopwatch and utters to himself: "Did you see that?"

Trainer Billy Turner remembers one such moment in his career, when Seattle Slew was barely a two-year-old.

"The first time I breezed him at Belmont, I knew he was an exceptional animal. He could fly." In that instant of recognition, Turner also knew what was required of him. "I shipped him back to the farm and didn't breeze him again for two months," he says. "He needed time to grow up."

For all the expense and energy that goes into the breeding, buying, and training of a thoroughbred, for all the glamour, prestige, and bloodlines, one thing ultimately makes the racing world turn: a horse's gift to run fast and hard and fearlessly. And for the men who are lucky enough to train such a horse, the challenge is to protect, nurture, and guide—and not to interfere.

After the summer sales, yearlings are sent to training centers to spend the late fall and winter in a climate where they can work out daily. While many training centers have been built in California and Florida, most of the old, established stables in the East use Aiken, South Carolina. Here trainers and horses converge for the first leg of a long journey to racing competition.

For both man and animal this is one of the most difficult and important times in a horse's development—a time when a wrong decision or a heavy hand can affect the horse's future. First, the yearling must learn to accept the feel of a bit, then a girth, and then the saddle and bridle. Eventually, once the horse is used to carry a rider, it can be taken for easy gallops around a small training track. His strength and stamina growing, by spring the two-year-old will be ready for gallops on a regulation-sized track.

During this time, a trainer begins to plan a strategy for the horse's racing career. Some two-year-olds show a proclivity for running on grass rather than dirt; some display more speed than stamina and will thus be groomed for shorter races rather than longer ones. It is the special skill of the experienced trainer that he can look at a horse's stride and conformation, judge his temperament, weigh his pedigree, and begin to tailor him for the competition for which he will be best suited. Veteran trainer John Veitch has worked for both Calumet Farm and Darby Dan, two of the most respected names in the business. He points out that "it's up to the trainer to identify a horse's style as soon as possible, then develop it. The best way to mess up a horse is to try to make him do something he's not capable of doing."

Fragile and injury prone at any age, as a two-year-old, a thoroughbred is entering into an area where the stresses are extraordinary, and where his competitive blood will drive him to his limits—and often beyond. One of the trainer's most difficult tasks is to shepherd his young horses into competition in good health. For two-year-olds the first real tests come in their third summer, and the showplace of two-year-old racing is Saratoga, New York.

Nestled in the foothills of the Adirondacks, four hours north of New York City and an hour north of Albany, Saratoga was a mecca for high society at the time of the Civil War. Famed for its health-inducing mineral spas, Saratoga offered a glittering array of nightlife, gambling casinos, and a racetrack. While many people still visit the area to partake in the mineral waters, the casinos have long since closed. Along with a host of summer cultural activities, horse racing is the main event.

Here, at a racetrack virtually unchanged in a hundred years, legends are born—or sunk. With the turn-of-the-century mansions on Union Avenue nearby, with its gardens of flowers and tall pine trees spilling shade for strolling picnickers and patrons, Saratoga is a state of mind. Around the paddocks and the backstretch, horse people gather to talk about promising young horses, and to recall such famous two-year-old races as the 1919 Sanford Stakes, in which one of the racing world's greatest legends suffered his only loss.

The horse was Man o' War, a big chestnut yearling from the Glen Riddle Farm of Samuel D. Riddle, and his jockey that day was one Johnny Loftus. At the bell, Loftus and Man o' War faltered and were far back in the early going. When Loftus finally found room to move, Man o' War began a powerful charge on the outside, but fell just short of catching the winner, who was aptly named Upset. Many of the crowd of 20,000 were disappointed in this horse about which much had been written and said. No one had any way of knowing that they had just witnessed the only race "Big Red" would ever lose. It was that race, along with the unpredictability of two-year-old racing in general, that lent Saratoga the nickname "The Graveyard of Favorites."

After the summer meet at Saratoga, with its festive and traditional atmosphere, the two-year-olds from the major eastern stables travel to Long Island for the top two-year-old races at Belmont Park, the Belmont Futurity and the Champagne. Until the $1 million Breeders' Cup Juvenile was established in 1984 in California, the Champagne was considered the ultimate two-year-old race of the year—and the one most likely to produce the early favorite for next year's Kentucky Derby.

The Champagne is a mile race, which is generally as far as trainers will allow their two-year-olds to run. Many of the early two-year-old races are only 5½ furlongs, less than three-quarters of a mile. As the young horses grow stronger and more mature, they are entered at longer distances. By the end of the season, trainers must have some idea of whether their charges are ready for the distances of next year's Triple Crown races—1¼ miles at the Derby, 1³⁄₁₆ at the Preakness, and a grueling 1½ at the Belmont Stakes.

Throughout the summer and fall meets, there is a great deal of pressure on trainers to establish their horse's racing prowess. As Saratoga convenes, the racing world is still fresh from the glamour of the Triple Crown races for three-year-olds. Pundits are looking for trends and early favorites for next year, and more than a few nervous owners are looking for some return on their investment. Thus, perhaps more than any other quality a trainer may have, patience is often the most difficult to maintain. It is also the most precious.

Good trainers are careful about judging their two-year-olds' early performances. In 1988, John Veitch won the Florida Derby with a horse named Brian's Time. The horse had fared poorly in the short two-year-old races the summer before. Another trainer might have given up on Brian's Time, but Veitch had suspected that the colt was still growing into his form. He stuck with Brian's Time and kept working with him, until the longer three-year-old races let him demonstrate his true ability.

Wealthier, established owners tend to allow their trainers this time to bring a horse along. In 1987, veteran trainer MacKenzie Miller brought along Java Gold so slowly for Paul Mellon's Rokeby Stable that the Kentucky Derby was never even considered. His patience was rewarded in August of Java Gold's three-year-old campaign, when he won the prestigious Travers Stakes at Saratoga over a field that included Alysheba, the winner of that year's Kentucky Derby and Preakness.

Owner Eugene V. Klein was also famous for his patience with young horses. Klein and his trainer, D. Wayne Lukas, sent their yearlings to Klein's 120-stall private training center in Rancho Sante Fe, California, just outside San Diego. There, Lukas studied Klein's "babies" and formed a strategy for each, while Klein watched the horses from his Spanish-style home on a hill overlooking the center.

In 1988, Klein told a *Sports Illustrated* interviewer that he wasn't in any hurry to get his horses to the track. "I like sitting in my office and looking out the window at the babies," Klein said. "Boy, it's great to have a love affair like this, especially in my later years."

But although Klein knew the value of patience with two-year-olds, an atmosphere of million-dollar purses and intense competition can get the better of anyone. In 1987, trainer Woody Stephens won the Champagne at Belmont with Forty Niner, a colt he trained for Claiborne Farm. Instead of going to California in November for the Breeders' Cup Juvenile—a newly established championship race—Stephens announced that he would race the colt once more, in the Breeders' Futurity at Keeneland, and wrap him up for the year. He wanted a rested horse for the 1988 Triple Crown campaign.

When a Klein-owned, Lukas-trained horse, Success Express, won the Breeders' Cup Juvenile that year, Klein publicly chided Stephens: "It's a shame that they didn't come to California to settle it [the two-year-old championship] properly."

But Klein, in Stephens's place, would have done the same thing. The next year Forty Niner finished a strong second in the Kentucky Derby and was one of the dominant horses of the year. The horse that beat him at Churchill Downs was, ironically, another Klein-owned horse, the filly Winning Colors. Once again, hers was a story of patience.

Winning Colors was purchased by Lukas and Klein for $575,000 at the Keeneland select summer sale two years earlier, the daughter of the imported stallion Caro. At Klein's training facility in California, Lukas faced a choice of keeping her in California or sending her to New York, where his horses are trained by his son, Jeff.

"Jeff and I were walking through the four barns of the two-year-olds at the training center, and when we got to the third barn, I told Jeff, 'Wait till you see this filly.' We brought out Winning Colors, and Jeff said, 'If I have a draft choice, I want this one.' I said. 'She's yours.' "

As a two-year-old, Winning Colors had only two races and wasn't even included in Lukas's five-horse entry in the $1-million Breeders' Cup Juvenile Fillies race. After she won the Kentucky Derby the following year, Lukas recalled: "The hardest thing we had to do when she was a two-year-old was keep her in the barn on Breeders' Cup day instead of sending her over there and saying, 'Hey, take a look at this.' We knew she was the best of the bunch, but that she needed time to develop."

Sometimes, however, a combination of a horse's precocious racing ability and the lure of competition make it impossible to keep a two-year-old in the barn. No two two-year-olds have ever created the rivalry and sheer racing electricity of Alydar and Affirmed in 1977.

Alydar was a big, long-striding colt trained by John Veitch for Calumet Farm, which had produced a record eight Kentucky Derby winners from Whirlaway in 1941 to Forward Pass in 1968. Alydar might have become Calumet's ninth Derby success, had it not been for a golden colt owned by financier Louis Wolfson and trained by Laz Barrera. Not quite as big or as striking as Alydar, Affirmed was a horse who simply refused to be beaten.

The two horses met each other six times as two-year-olds—four times at Belmont Park, once at Saratoga, and once at Laurel in Maryland. Of those races, Affirmed won four, Alydar two. In two victories, Affirmed's winning margins were a nose and a neck. When their extraordinary two-year-old campaign was over, the racing world waited to see what would happen during the 1978 Triple Crown.

But Louis Wolfson was apprehensive. Late in 1977, Wolfson approached a third party—Leslie Combs II of Spendthrift Farm—to see if Calumet would be interested in selling Alydar. Wolfson said later, "I didn't feel these two colts should keep racing against each other, and if I had been able to obtain Alydar, I would have run them in different races." A week later, Combs reported back to Wolfson: Calumet's owners, Admiral and Mrs. Gene Markey, were not interested in selling their star colt.

The following year Alydar and Affirmed picked up their rivalry where they had left off. In the Kentucky Derby, Affirmed's margin of victory was 1½ lengths. In the Preakness, he won by a neck, and in the Belmont, by a head. There had never been a Triple Crown duel like it. Here were two horses who had come to maturity at the same time, stayed healthy, and pushed each other to their very limits. In a sport where bloodlines are studied and carefully mixed, where millions of dollars are spent and training is painstaking and precise, it was a drama of sheer racing destiny that no human being could possibly have created or foretold.

AMERICA'S TRIPLE CROWN is a coronation for the thoroughbred world. Worth millions of dollars in purse money, the Triple Crown establishes the best horses, most dominant bloodlines, and most successful farms. In three spectacular races, a supreme order comes to a world that is often hectic and confusing.

But despite its preeminence, the Triple Crown is only the culmination of another series of races. Known as the "prep" races, these high-stakes contests are themselves a gathering of racing royalty, for only the best of the top three-year-olds are entered. Besides giving racing's powers-that-be a way of selecting entries for the Kentucky Derby, the Preakness, and the Belmont Stakes, the prep races give the public a chance to get to know the season's elite horses, to pick their favorites, and to establish the emotional ties that make the sport more than a sport, and the Triple Crown more than a series of horse races.

At the beginning of each racing year, trainers and owners map a special, Triple Crown strategy for their leading horses. Most want to win the Kentucky Derby, but some look ahead to the Preakness or the Belmont. In recent years, the huge purses offered by the new Breeders' Cup races later in the season have provided another option for horsemen with immature or slow-developing horses.

To get to the Derby, a horse must finish in the top twenty in earnings in graded stakes races. (Often, due to injury or illness, the final number of race-day entries is less.) The way an owner and trainer make that exclusive field of twenty is by first nominating their horse for consideration, and then entering the major prep races—choosing those races in which their horses will have the best chance of doing well.

Normally, trainers of the big stables not only nominate their best three-year-olds, but also unproven colts and fillies who have shown any spark of potential. By nominating virtually all of their horses, they can avoid the sort of embarrassment that D. Wayne Lukas experienced in 1980.

At that time, Lukas, a former quarterhorse trainer, was still relatively new to the thoroughbred game. His public stable included two colts owned by Tartan Farm of Florida, the operation that campaigned the brilliant Dr. Fager in the late 1960s. Tartan boss John Nerud was wary of the Kentucky Derby—regarding it as too long a course too early in the year. So Lukas decided to nominate only the strongest, most mature of his two Tartan colts, Idyll.

In the weeks after his nomination, however, the other Tartan Farm horse, Codex, began to develop. Entered into the Hollywood Derby as a prohibitive long shot, he won a startling victory. Such a win, for any other horse, would have made him an immediate Kentucky Derby favorite. Alas for Lukas, Codex was unnominated. He spent Derby day in his barn in California while the filly Genuine Risk was upsetting the colts at Churchill Downs. Under the rules in effect at that time, Lukas was able to enter Codex in the Preakness. It was both an occasion of great joy and some bitterness for Lukas when Codex won the second leg of the Triple Crown by 4½ lengths over Genuine Risk.

The major Triple Crown prep races are held in Florida, California, New York, Louisiana, Arkansas, and Kentucky. The trainer's task of matching his horses with each race, getting the right competition, and avoiding fields or individual horses requires skillful maneuvering and not a little guile. Trainers fear having a promising but still-developing horse in a race he cannot succeed in, tiring a good horse out in distances he is not ready for, or getting caught up in an unnecessary confrontation with a horse whose style of running could be detrimental to his own. Injury and illness, of course, are ever-present dangers. Generally, trainers like to gradually lead a horse into longer and longer races, moving up to a mile and an eighth—only a furlong shorter than the Kentucky Derby. Some trainers prefer their final prep to come in Kentucky, to help a horse get used to the weather and atmosphere that will prevail at Churchill Downs. But as with all rules of thumb in horse racing, there are the beguiling exceptions. For two Derby winners of the 1980s—Ferdinand and Sunday Silence—the Derby was their first race outside California.

In recent years, California has become an increasingly dominant horse-racing region. Besides being a home base for such outstanding trainers as Charlie Whittingham, Laz Barrera, D. Wayne Lukas, and Jack Van Berg—who each trained at least one Kentucky Derby winner between 1978 and 1989—California's leading parks, Santa Anita and Hollywood, offer luxurious purses to match their perfect weather. Today, many of the leading jockeys live year-round in California.

The top Triple Crown prep race in California is the Santa Anita Derby, a mile-and-an-eighth race that generally comes a month before the Kentucky Derby. With its swaying palm trees and ornate clubhouse and Turf Club, Santa Anita is a lovely track situated by the San Gabriel Mountains. The Derby always draws an enormous crowd that includes many of the film and television industry's most famous stars.

For trainers who don't relish California's tough competition, the South offers two Triple Crown prep races—the Louisiana Derby at the New Orleans Fair Grounds, and the Arkansas Derby at Oaklawn Park in Hot Springs, Arkansas.

All of the major prep races have their own unique flavor and atmosphere, and the Louisiana and Arkansas are no exception. The Fair Grounds draws a varied, colorful crowd, the kind of crowd that enjoys its racing by day and French Quarter pleasures by night. The Arkansas is a traditional, down-home affair, a sort of pleasant, wholesome picnic in the country. Purses and prestige for both races have grown over the years. Although no Louisiana Derby winner had won the Kentucky Derby since Black Gold in 1924, that race received a boost in 1988 when Risen Star finished a strong third at Churchill Downs before going on to win the Preakness and Belmont. The Arkansas Derby never had a Kentucky Derby winner until 1983, when Sunny's Halo turned the trick. In 1984 and 1987, the Arkansas produced two Kentucky Derby favorites in Althea and Demons Begone.

For eastern horsemen, the traditional road to the Triple Crown begins in Florida at Hialeah Park near Miami, and at Gulfstream Park, north of Miami and closer to Ft. Lauderdale. Here, from late winter to early spring, some of the best prep races in America are run every year.

Hialeah is a track unmatched in opulence. Built in 1925, it features sweeping marble staircases, wide verandas, towering palms, and a flock of flamingos on an infield lake. Long a winter playground for New York socialites and racing's old-money families, Hialeah offers such important stakes races as the Everglades and the Flamingo, the culmination of its three-year-old Triple Crown prep races. In 1948, Calumet Farm's Citation swept his way to greatness by winning four races at Hialeah on his way to capturing the Triple Crown.

In the early 1950s, Gulfstream Park began to challenge Hialeah as the best winter racing spot on the East Coast. Located within sight of the Atlantic Ocean in the town of Hallandale, Gulfstream gave horsemen another important prep race when it inaugurated the Florida Derby in 1952. Through 1988, the Florida Derby produced fourteen winners in the Kentucky Derby, fifteen in the Preakness, and ten in the Belmont. Besides being a great race, the Florida Derby is a happening. Every year it offers a panoply of beauty queens, marching bands, an official drink called the Derby Daiquiri, purple orchids, and usually a wild-animal race involving zebras, camels, or ostriches. Besides the sideshows over the years, perhaps the most memorable Derby itself was the 1979 effort of Spectacular Bid. In that race, Spectacular Bid labored under a misguided effort by his jockey, young Ron Franklin. Coming from far back in the pack, Spectacular Bid seemed suddenly to make up his own mind on how to run his race. Spectators later swore that they could actually see the horse overcoming his jockey's ineptitude, and at the wire the colt finished ahead by an astounding 4½ lengths.

From Florida, the surviving Triple Crown contenders usually go to New York for the Wood Memorial at Aqueduct, or to Kentucky for the Blue Grass Stakes at Keeneland. Both are mile-and-an-eighth preps that have traditionally been the final tune-ups for many Derby winners. Deciding which to run in often depends on how much time a trainer thinks his horse needs between his last prep and the Kentucky Derby. The Wood comes exactly two weeks before the Derby. The Blue Grass was only nine days beforehand until 1989, when it was moved back to three weeks before Derby Day.

One of the most unusual Wood Memorials of recent years was in 1973. The favorite was Secretariat, who had won the two-year-old championship and had already been syndicated for stud duty for $6.08 million, then a world record. In the Wood, however, Secretariat struggled across the finish line in third. Although most spectators realized that he had been caught in heavy traffic, some syndicate members suffered an attack of nerves. In a bravura, gentlemanly gesture, breeder Seth Hancock of Claiborne Farm offered to refund investors' money. Some syndicate members accepted his offer, while others stuck with the horse. In the following weeks, Secretariat became the first horse in twenty-five years to win the Triple Crown, demolishing the field in the Belmont by 31 lengths.

All the major prep races have their side stories and their own small legends. For the Blue Grass Stakes, people who were there will always remember 1978, when Calumet Farm's Alydar ran his final prep race before meeting Affirmed in the Triple Crown. That was the last time that Calumet's owners, Admiral and Mrs. Gene Markey, were to see a Calumet horse win a race in person.

Calumet Farm has produced more Kentucky Derby winners (eight) than any other breeding farm. Throughout the forties and fifties Calumet virtually dominated the world of thoroughbred racing.

In 1978, the Markeys were in declining health. They had been following their horses on television, and using the telephone to communicate with their trainers. For the 1978 Blue Grass Stakes, Keeneland president James E. "Ted" Bassett arranged to have the Markeys brought to trackside to watch their best horse, Alydar, run.

The Markeys arrived in a station wagon, which was parked next to the rail at the top of the homestretch until the horses came on the track. Ordinarily, the horses turn right and parade past the grandstand. This day, though, they turned left and were led past the clubhouse toward the Markeys.

As the horses began to file past, Admiral and Mrs. Markey were helped out of the car. Alydar was the seventh and last horse to come by. As he arrived, the Markeys were on their feet, leaning against the rail. Mrs. Markey wore white gloves, traditional apparel for a Kentucky lady on a racing day.

Jockey Jorge Velasquez, the great Panamanian-born rider, was aboard Alydar. As he passed the elderly couple, he tipped his cap.

"Hello, my lady," he said to Mrs. Markey. "How have you been doing? Here's your baby. Don't he look pretty?"

At Admiral Markey's request, Velasquez brought Alydar closer to the rail. For a moment, while the crowd looked on from the grandstand, the strong, glistening young horse and the elderly couple stood face-to-face, lost in their moment. Then Velasquez took the colt to the post.

The Markeys sat in their car until the race began. Then, as the field entered the turn for home, they came back to the rail, and Mrs. Markey gripped the rail with her white gloves. Just then, amidst the pounding of hooves, the flying dirt, and the roar of the grandstand, Alydar swept past, taking the lead.

Mrs. Markey smiled at the sight. Perhaps she thought of other great Calumet horses, of Whirlaway or Citation or Tim Tam. Or perhaps she was only happy to be there, to see the farm's red and blue silks on their way to victory.

Nine days later, Affirmed denied Alydar's bid to win a ninth Kentucky Derby for Calumet. And within two years of that Blue Grass Stakes at Keeneland, a new generation had taken the reins of Calumet Farm. Both the lady in the white gloves and her husband were gone.

EVERY YEAR, ONE DAY A YEAR, the sport of horse racing becomes America's sport. On this day, from New York to California, people stop and ask each other, "Who do you like in the Derby?" Television sets show images of crowded grandstands, jockeys in brightly colored silks, a winner's circle filled with smiling faces and roses. . . . On this day, all the hard, behind-the-scenes work that goes into the sport, all the early-morning, winter workouts, the muddy backstretches and sweaty tack rooms, vanish behind a panoply of the sights, sounds, and legends. This is Kentucky Derby day. Along with the Preakness, Belmont, and Breeders' Cup, this is a day when even the most casual racing fan may lose his heart to a great horse, and when a new racing legend may be born.

How does such an event come to be? How does a single horse race make its way into the fabric of the nation? In the case of the Kentucky Derby, the answer lies in the perseverance of the men and women who make the sport their lives, and the magic of tradition itself.

In 1872, in the state of Kentucky, horse racing was virtually moribund. There had not been a major stakes race since the Civil War, and a number of thoroughbred breeders were considering closing their farms. As a last-ditch effort, a consortium of breeders came to M. Lewis Clark, a young entrepreneur who was a nephew of Louisville's founder, George Rogers Clark, and grandson of William Clark, half of the famous expeditionary team of Lewis and Clark. The horsemen asked Clark to come up with a way to save racing in the Bluegrass State. Clark took up the challenge.

A big, balding man who eventually grew to a weight of 300 pounds, Clark knew what he wanted. He envisioned a single event that would galvanize the public's imagination—and a new, glamorous track to stage it on. Traveling to Europe, he studied the great tracks and races of England and France. When he returned, he had his plans: a race modeled after England's Epsom Derby. Leasing 180 acres just south of Louisville's city limits from the Churchill family, Clark put together an investment group of 320 patrons at $100 each and began construction on his track. When the cost of building and the leveling of the rough terrain exhausted his $32,000, Clark received a donation from Major W. H. Thomas, a prominent Louisville businessman, to complete the grandstand and stables on what is now the backside of the Downs.

The first Kentucky Derby was held in 1875 and won by a horse named Aristides. In Louisville, the race was pronounced a great social and artistic success, but for the rest of the country, the event would take some time and doing for them to discover. Indeed, it would take the efforts of a special man to make the Derby great.

That man was Col. Matt Winn, and his particular genius was for publicity. In 1902, Winn bought Churchill Downs to save the track and the race from going out of business. Thereupon, the pudgy, cigar-chomping promoter devoted his life to his Derby.

Winn called the Derby "The Greatest Two Minutes in Sports" and he hounded the sportswriters who covered it. In the off-season, he established a headquarters in New York so he could rub shoulders with such powerful sports columnists as Damon Runyon, Grantland Rice, and Bill Corum—men whose bylines, in a golden age of newspapers, were read from coast to coast.

The writers fell in love with Winn. Unabashedly he plied them with free quotes and free drinks. His policy was simple and direct: "Give me the five best writers in New York, and you can have the rest." While Winn was around, no sportswriter ever picked up a check.

Of course, public relations alone could not make the Kentucky Derby into America's most-watched horse race, and Winn was helped by a string of fortuitous events on the track itself. In 1913, the winning horse was Donerail—a colossal upset paying $184.90 for a $2 bet. In 1914, the track record was smashed by a gelding named Old Rosebud. In 1915, Harry Payne Whitney's Regret became the first filly to "win the roses." Winn had a field day when Whitney told the press: "This is the greatest race in America at the present time, and I don't care if she [Regret] ever starts again."

As the Derby grew in stature, purses, and popularity, its success helped buoy two other races held soon after it: the Preakness in Baltimore and the Belmont Stakes in New York. Although no one is exactly sure who invented the term—some give credit to the late Charles Hatton of the *Daily Racing Form*—these three races were grouped together during the 1920s to form a spring series referred to as the "Triple Crown." The notion of a three-round contest for racing supremacy caught on with the public and the press. Research revealed that only one horse had ever won all three races—Sir Barton in 1919. Once the Triple Crown concept was officially established, Gallant Fox was the second Triple Crown champion in 1930. Between that year and the end of the 1980s, only eleven horses had ever been good enough—and lucky enough—to win the Triple Crown.

Col. Matt Winn died in 1949, just before the dawn of the television age. In 1956, a group of Louisville civic leaders founded the Kentucky Derby Festival, which went on to become a ten-day celebration of luncheons, parties, and races for everything from runners to hot-air balloons to steamboats. The Kentucky Derby, fueled by worldwide attention, had hit full stride. By the mid-1980s, the track received a $25-million renovation and reconstruction program designed to add more modern facilities, while maintaining the look and atmosphere of Churchill's hallowed past.

Every year more than 1,200 reporters—many of whom will not cover another horse race the rest of the year—converge on Churchill Downs to write about the Derby. Nicknamed the "Dawn Patrol" by the horsemen who have to face them, the reporters swarm over the barn area in search of an interesting angle or a fresh perspective. For most of the year, trainers work in obscurity. Now they find themselves fielding questions from novice turf writers, like the one asked by a Detroit reporter in 1979, when a son of Secretariat named General Assembly was running in the Derby: "If Secretariat saw him, would he recognize him?" It is a part of racing life that most grizzled horsemen are content with facing only a few times a year.

For all of the modern media's power, for all the beautiful pictures and stirring words, the Derby has been its own best promoter by consistently offering great performances, stunning upsets, and a flair for controversy. In 1933, it was the famous "Fighting Finish" between jockeys Don Meade and Herb Fisher. In 1953, the immortal Native Dancer suffered what was to be the only loss of his career. In 1957, jockey Bill Shoemaker misjudged the finish line aboard Gallant Man. Standing up in his stirrups, Shoemaker opened the way for Calumet Farm's Iron Leige to steal the victory. In one of the great mysteries of Derby history, Dancer's Image became the first and only Derby winner to be disqualified when a then-illegal medication was reported in his postrace tests in 1968. To this day, no one has ever admitted to giving the colt anything.

Every Derby has had a moment, or personality, that gives it an identity of its own. In 1966, it was jockey Don Brumfield proclaiming, "I'm the happiest hillbilly hardboot in the world," after his winning ride aboard Kauai King. In 1971, it was Canonero II, who was shipped from Venezuela on a plane loaded with chickens. The 1974 Derby had a royal touch, when Princess Margaret of Great Britain was the honored guest.

More than anything, the Derby has come to mean the celebration of tradition itself. No matter what changes have occurred in the world, every year on the first Saturday in May a crowd will come to Churchill Downs to watch a horse race. There will be the playing of "My Old Kentucky Home," mint juleps, the flower gardens of spring, the show business celebrities, the memories of races past. Made special by its setting, the race does honor to a part of the world that has served as a cradle for great racing horses.

Nevertheless, the Derby is not without its detractors. Many knowledgeable horsemen insist the race—at a mile and a quarter—is too long and too soon for still-developing three-year-olds. Some owners have turned a cold shoulder to the race, as did Samuel D. Riddle, who refused to enter Man o' War in 1920. In 1967, trainer Johnny Nerud of Florida's Tartan Farm bypassed the Derby with his great Dr. Fager.

In 1961, Jack Price was one such Derby doubter. A hard-bitten horseman with a fine horse named Carry Back, Price came to Louisville with undisguised scorn for all the hoopla and sentimental ceremony. As far as Price was concerned, it was just another horse race.

When the gates opened for the start of that Kentucky Derby, Carry Back got off slowly. Going into the final turn, the colt seemed hopelessly beaten. As famed announcer Bryan Field breathlessly told his audience around the country, "Carry Back too far back. . . . Can't make it unless he hurries." To everyone's amazement, hurry Carry Back did—until in the final strides, he passed Crozier to win by three-quarters of a length. Suddenly, Jack Price had discovered the Derby mystique.

From then on, Price has been one of the Derby's leading boosters. He comes to Churchill Downs every spring, spreading the story of a humble colt named Carry Back who raced to immortality on the first Saturday in May. When Carry Back died, twenty-two years after his Derby victory, the horse was buried under a shade tree outside the Kentucky Derby Museum. At the ceremony later, Price sipped a glass of champagne and talked about what the Derby meant to him.

"You can win all the Laurel Futuritys or Arlington Handicaps in the world," he said, "but they don't mean anything compared to the Derby. When you meet somebody on a plane and tell them you're in horse racing, all they want to know is if you've ever won the Kentucky Derby."

With the words "Carry Back too far back. . . . Can't make it unless he hurries" still echoing in his memory, it's a question Jack Price will always be ready to answer.

IN 1980, GENUINE RISK was the second filly in history to win the Kentucky Derby. Two weeks later, she was making a dramatic charge into the homestretch of the second Triple Crown race, the Preakness. What happened during that stretch run was a matter of much debate. Codex, under jockey Angel Cordero, Jr., had been leading the field. As Risk moved outside to challenge for the lead, Cordero glanced over his shoulder, then moved Codex to the outside, effectively forcing Genuine Risk out of the path she was running in. Her momentum broken, Genuine Risk was unable to recover, and Codex pulled off to a 4¾-length victory.

Genuine Risk's jockey, Jacinto Vasquez, immediately complained that he had been fouled. The stewards posted the objection sign, and former jockey Eddie Arcaro, doing the color commentary on national television, announced for the whole world to hear that Codex should be disqualified. But after reviewing the race films the stewards let the order of finish stand. The filly's owners, Mr. and Mrs. Bert Firestone, appealed to the state racing commission; the decision was upheld.

For all its attendant glamour and spectacle, when it comes to two thundering minutes around a track, horse racing is a tough and gritty business. If the Kentucky Derby has a way of displaying the glamorous side of the sport, the Preakness, run two weeks later at Pimlico racetrack just outside of Baltimore, Maryland, has a way of getting things back to basics.

At a mile and three-sixteenths, the Preakness is the shortest of the Triple Crown races. Without the Derby's old Kentucky atmosphere and the Belmont's big-city style, the Preakness has always had to struggle to maintain its own identity among the Triple Crown races. But because it is the second leg of the trio, the Preakness has a built-in sense of drama. The Derby having been run, one horse comes to Pimlico with the unique opportunity to pursue the Triple Crown dream—while a whole field of horses has the opportunity to stop him.

Named for the horse that won Pimlico's first stakes race in 1870, the Preakness gained prominence in the early part of the century. By 1920, the race had more prestige in the East than the Derby itself. (It was to save Man o' War for the Preakness—which he went on to win—that owner Samuel D. Riddle kept the colt out of the Derby in 1920.) As the Kentucky Derby became the dominant race in the thirties, the Preakness found itself in eclipse. What the race needed was a good promoter. It found him in Pimlico's general manager, Chick Lang.

Lang was a congenial, portly man known for his sense of humor and crew cut. The son of a jockey who had won the 1928 Kentucky Derby with Reigh Count, Lang became the Preakness's number one supporter. Derby week in Louisville was Lang's favorite time to do his job. At parties and press conferences, he went around attaching small, embroidered black-eyed Susans—the Preakness flower—to every lapel that stood still long enough to be pinned, all the while referring to the Derby as "Preakness prep." Once Lang rented a lighted billboard in downtown Louisville to advertise the Preakness during the Derby Festival parade.

Between 1960 and 1981, partly due to Lang's efforts, every Derby winner ran in the Preakness. But in the eighties, Lang and Pimlico ran into trouble. In 1982, coowner Arthur B. Hancock and trainer

Eddie Gregson announced that they were skipping the Preakness so they could point Derby winner Gato Del Sol toward the Belmont. Stung, Lang went on the attack. He put a padlock on the door of the Preakness barn usually reserved for the Derby winner, and he publicly mocked both Gato Del Sol and Gregson.

"I think Eddie what's his name owes something to the horse business," Lang said. "He has the only horse that has a chance to be a Triple Crown winner. If this colt wins the Belmont, there will be a lot of days when he'll be shaving and he'll be glad he's got an electric razor in his hand instead of a straight razor."

Lang's emotional tirades did not sway Gregson's plans. After Aloma's Ruler won the Preakness, the well-rested Gato Del Sol ran in the Belmont, where he finished far back of Conquistador Cielo.

In 1983, peace was restored at Pimlico when Sunny's Halo was brought on to Baltimore after his Derby win. But two years later, Lang was on the warpath again.

In 1985, a prominent New Jersey investment banker, Robert Brennan, decided that the way to revive New Jersey racing would be to put up a $2-million bonus for any horse able to sweep the Cherry Hill Mile, Garden State Stakes, Kentucky Derby, and the Jersey Derby. In a sport not adverse to public relations gimmicks, this one was a beauty. What made Brennan's offer particularly enticing, though, was that a horse quickly accomplished the first half of the trick.

The horse was Spend a Buck, owned by Dennis Diaz and purchased for a paltry $12,500. After winning the Cherry Hill Mile and the Garden State Stakes, Spend a Buck won a sizzling wire-to-wire victory in the Derby. Diaz was faced with a historic decision. Should he go for the Preakness and the Triple Crown's tradition, or for the Jersey Derby and Brennan's $2 million? He went for the money— and the racing establishment was shaken to its foundation. Naturally, Lang led the charge. "A snake-oil salesman" was one of the kinder labels he pinned on Brennan, who responded by giving the name to one of his own horses.

Spend a Buck went on to win both the Jersey Derby and Horse of the Year honors. The Triple Crown responded by coming up with a $5-million bonus of its own for any horse able to sweep all three classics. And in the absence of the Triple Crown winner, the horse with the best overall finishes in the three races would get a $1-million bonus. Since Spend a Buck, every Derby winner has gone on to Pimlico.

In 1986, Pimlico's owners, Ben and Herman Cohen, sold the track to Frank J. De Francis. Lang, so long the champion of the Preakness, went to work for the newly formed Triple Crown Productions, where his main job was to gather entries for all three races early in the year.

Today, the Preakness retains its unique character. It is a race that lacks the Derby's spectacle but exemplifies the fury and competitiveness of the sport; a race held in a colorful and easy-going, unpretentious atmosphere.

On the third Saturday in May, crowds of more than 80,000 make their way up the expressways and along the narrow neighborhood streets surrounding the old track. Many of the fans are teenagers and college students who head for the infield to throw Frisbees, listen to rock bands, play soccer, and work on their tans. Unlike at Churchill Downs, where the horses are saddled in a paddock behind the grandstand, at the Preakness horses are led down the track and onto the infield, where they are saddled on the grass in full view of the crowd. At the center of the infield is the old cupola that once sat atop the original Pimlico clubhouse, destroyed by fire in 1966. When the race has been run, and the results are official, a painter climbs a ladder to the top of the cupola and paints the weather vane with the winning owner's colors.

The Preakness not only means great racing, it means Maryland crab cakes, sight-seeing trips to places such as Fort McHenry and Annapolis, or tickets to a Baltimore Orioles' home game.

As with all great races, every fan has his favorite Preakness. Many will remember Secretariat's sensational move on the first turn, when he went from last to first under jockey Ron Turcotte. On his way to becoming the first Triple Crown winner in twenty-five years, Secretariat apparently broke the Preakness record, only to have his time erased because of a malfunction in the official timer. Five years later, many observers believed they had seen the best race in Preakness history when jockey Steve Cauthen got Affirmed a neck ahead of Alydar at the wire—and left the crowd drained with excitement.

Between 1979 and 1983 the Preakness was won three times by Baltimore-owned horses: Spectacular Bid in 1979, Aloma's Ruler in 1982, and Deputed Testamony [sic] in 1983. Nevertheless, the eighties will best be remembered both by the Genuine Risk–Codex controversy, and an even more bitter one that erupted in 1988, again involving another Kentucky Derby–winning filly, Winning Colors.

Ironically, D. Wayne Lukas, who had trained Codex in 1980, was involved again—only this time it was his horse who was carried out of the race. The offender this time was the highly touted colt Forty Niner, who had finished second in the Derby. When the starting gate opened in the Preakness, Forty Niner, under jockey Pat Day, ran a race that seemed designed more to exhaust Winning Colors than to win the race itself. Afterward—the race was won by Risen Star—Winning Colors' owner, Eugene V. Klein, engaged in an extraordinary public attack against Forty Niner's trainer, Woody Stephens, and jockey Day. Klein accused the Stephens team of a vendetta, of trying to break up the filly's Triple Crown bid. Curiously, Lukas kept silent on the matter, perhaps remembering his part in the Codex affair eight years before.

So goes Maryland's entry in the Triple Crown, a race that seems to bring out the fighting spirit in everyone involved. Perhaps the 1962 Preakness best displayed the essence of the contest. That was the year that Ridan, with Manuel Ycaza in the irons, and Greek Money, under Johnny Rotz, dueled head-to-head down the stretch. A head-on photograph of the stretch run, taken by Joseph A. DiPaola and considered one of the great racing shots ever taken, showed Ycaza leaning into Rotz, his left elbow virtually touching Greek Money's head.

Nevertheless, it was Greek Money who got a nose in front at the wire. Unaware that he had been captured for posterity by DiPaola's camera, the audacious Ycaza immediately claimed that he had been fouled during the race. Reviewing the race film, the stewards declared the race official. After further examination of the films, they fined Ycaza $200 and suspended him for ten days for rough riding.

OF THE ELEVEN HORSES that have managed to win the Triple Crown, only one has earned a permanent place at New York's Belmont Park. The horse is Secretariat, and his statue, situated in the middle of the track's walking ring, casts a long shadow.

It was at Belmont Park in 1973 that Secretariat became the ninth winner of the Triple Crown. For those who saw the race, at the track and on television nationwide, there can be no forgetting the big chestnut colt's performance.

On a beautiful June day, Secretariat ran a mile and a half in 2:24 seconds, a track record that stands to this day. His margin of victory was an astounding 31 lengths. Uncontested, he crossed the wire going away, as if he were competing against himself, arrogantly testing the far limits of his own speed and strength. Television viewers would not forget track announcer Chic Anderson's words as the race unfolded:

"Secretariat by twelve, Secretariat by fourteen, Secretariat is moving like a tremendous machine."

It was the most spectacular effort of one of racing's truly legendary competitors—the first horse to grace the cover of *Time* and *Newsweek,* and to play to the public in the age of television. It was, what's more, an effort that will haunt every Belmont Stakes that is ever run.

Today, the Belmont remains not only the final leg of the Triple Crown, but also the crown jewel of thoroughbred racing in New York. Fittingly, it is a race of extraordinary challenge.

New York has long been a home base for some of the nation's finest stables, best horsemen, and most competitive racing, and Belmont Park is the hub of New York racing. Renovated in 1966, Belmont is a sprawling oasis of stables and tracks that lies just outside the New York City limits in Elmont, Long Island. With its shade trees and magnificent grandstand, the track provides a beautiful setting for the culmination of the Triple Crown drama. Ironically, however, because of New York's busy sports and social calendar, the Belmont Stakes never makes the impression on its hometown that the Derby does on Louisville, or the Preakness on Baltimore. The Belmont produces no parades and little pageantry. What it does provide is a grueling mile and a half known as the "Test of Champions."

Hall of Fame trainer Woody Stephens is a leading advocate of New York racing and the Belmont in particular. "You haven't done anything until you've done it in New York," he likes to tell rivals. It's a position he can afford to take, for New York has been very good to Stephens. From 1982 through 1986, he dominated the Belmont Stakes.

A successful New York–based trainer since the late 1940s, Stephens won the Belmont an unheard of five straight times, a record that some racing people rank on a par with Joe DiMaggio's 56-game hitting streak in baseball and UCLA's ten national collegiate basketball championships in twelve years. Stephens's five winning horses were all different in ability and temperament. Of the five, Conquistador Cielo in 1982, Caveat in '83, Swale in '84, Creme Fraiche in '85, and Danzig Connection in '86, only one—Swale—was able to win another Triple Crown race.

Many three-year-olds come into the Belmont never having raced at a mile and a half before. To be successful in the Belmont, a horse must be in top physical form, have the right combination of stamina and speed, and be perfectly guided by his jockey on race day. Few trainers can ever be sure how their young horse will do at the new distance in the intense competition, and the race is famous for bringing out hidden weaknesses—or hidden greatness. Such greatness was brought out in Alydar and Affirmed in 1978.

After their dramatic two-year-old racing season, Affirmed had established a 4–2 advantage over his rival. Yet invariably, the final margin was less than a half-length either way. As three-year-olds, both came to the Kentucky Derby unbeaten for the year; Alydar the best in the East, Affirmed in the West.

In the Derby, Alydar's late charge came just short of catching Affirmed. In the Preakness, the two engaged in their thrilling stretch duel, with Affirmed once more coming out ahead. Many believed that the Belmont would give Alydar the distance he needed to overtake his nemesis at last.

At Belmont, Alydar made his move on Affirmed less than halfway through the race. From there on, to the crowd's delight and astonishment, the two rivals slugged it out like heavyweight champions, head-to-head, heart-to-heart. Said Affirmed's trainer, Laz Barrera, later, "Alydar, he fought like a tiger. As long as I live, I never see two horses fight like this."

Near the three-sixteenths pole, Alydar finally seemed to get his nose in front. But then Affirmed's eighteen-year-old jockey, Steve Cauthen, did something he had never done to the horse before. Hemmed in by Jorge Velasquez on Alydar, desperately searching for a winning edge, Cauthen used a trick he had practiced while straddling bales of hay on his family's Kentucky farm. He deftly switched his whip from his right hand to his left and whipped the colt on.

With Cauthen flailing with his left hand and Velasquez with his right, the two horses strained for the finish. When they hit the wire, Affirmed was in front by a head.

And so Affirmed joined the select group of horses who'd managed to cap victories at the Kentucky Derby and the Preakness with a win at Belmont: Sir Barton in 1919, Gallant Fox in 1930, Omaha in 1935, War Admiral in 1937, Whirlaway in 1941, Count Fleet in 1943, Assault in 1946, Citation in 1948, Secretariat in 1973, and Seattle Slew in 1977. In addition, a new legend had been born: of the soft-spoken eighteen-year-old jockey in the pink and black silks who had the composure to switch whip hands down the stretch.

While eleven horses have captured the Triple Crown, the Belmont has been the undoing of another select group: fourteen times one horse has won the Kentucky Derby and the Preakness, only to be turned back in New York.

One of those was Canonero II. Purchased for $1,200 as a yearling, Canonero II raced in Venezuela and California as a two-year-old. When owner Edgar Caibett decided to ship him to Kentucky for the Derby, Canonero II traveled on a plane with farm animals. Upon his arrival in Louisville, trainer Juan Arias sent the horse on long, leisurely gallops instead of demanding speed drills. Dismissed by horsemen and bettors alike, Canonero II was good enough to run to a 3¾-length win at the Derby, and he went on to polish off the Preakness field in similar fashion.

Canonero II came to New York on a wave of publicity. Some observers called him suspect, while others hailed him as a wonder horse. New York's Latin community was excited over the prospect of a South American horse, with a South American jockey and owner, capturing the Triple Crown. In the days before the Belmont, however, Canonero II fell ill. After some debate, owner Caibett decided to race him anyway, and a record Belmont Stakes crowd of 82,000 shoved its way to the track. The day took on a decidedly Latin flavor, with flamenco dancers and the beat of maracas. In the race itself, the game Canonero II could only manage to struggle home fourth.

At Esposito's Tavern across from Belmont's back stable gate, where the picket fence is always painted with the Belmont winner's colors, patrons like to remember Canonero II and other great Belmont races. The jukebox at Esposito's even features a song called "The Seattle Slew Do-Dah," in honor of Seattle Slew and his trainer, Billy Turner, who frequented Esposito's during Slew's Triple Crown run in 1977.

No matter what horse captures the fancy of the Belmont faithful, there will never be any real argument about the singularly most remarkable Belmont performance. It is a mark of Secretariat's dominance that fifteen years after his record-setting race, he was once again a focal point of a Belmont Stakes when Risen Star became the first son of Secretariat to do battle in the Triple Crown races.

Bred by Arthur Hancock III at his Stone Farm, Risen Star was sold as a two-year-old to the partnership of Louis Roussel, whose father owned the New Orleans Fair Grounds racetrack, and Ronnie Lamarque, a New Orleans car dealer and part-time lounge singer. After dominating the major Kentucky Derby preps in Louisiana, the big colt was entered in the Lexington Stakes, where he earned his trip to the Derby by upsetting Forty Niner, then the Derby favorite.

During the Triple Crown campaign, the unorthodox Roussel became known as "Screwy Louie." Roussel was behind such events as a jockey tryout before the Derby, a near scratch before the Preakness, and a clock-stopping workout before the Belmont—all of which made bettors extremely wary. Risen Star, however, did not seem to mind his owner's tactics. Caught in early traffic problems in the Derby, he finished third. In the Preakness, he ran to victory when Forty Niner exhausted the favored Winning Colors in their controversial speed duel.

For the Belmont, Risen Star saved the best for last. His winning time of 2:26⅖ was second only to Secretariat's 1973 record, and his winning margin of 14½ lengths tied for the third biggest ever.

Magnificent in its own right, Risen Star's performance seemed to many to reflect only more glory on his sire. The statue on the island of trees and shrubbery inside Belmont's walking circle has that special magic about it. It says that in a business of competition there are some moments that can never be competed against. It says that there are some days, such as the one in June, in 1973, that will never fade away.

ON APRIL 23, 1982, a breeder named John Gaines received the Silver Horseshoe Award at the annual "They're Off" luncheon that kicks off the Kentucky Derby Festival in Louisville. In his acceptance speech, Gaines made a historic proposal, pointing out that while the breeding business was booming, racing itself was in a downswing. As yearling sales were rocketing toward a record $13.1 million for a single horse, racetracks around the country were reporting lowered attendance and wagering. The time had come, Gaines said, for the breeders to help the racing part of the industry by reinvesting some of their profits back into the sport.

Gaines had a plan. "We are looking at a single person that's the racing fan—the two-dollar bettor," he said. "He is the person we are trying to reach and whose imagination we are trying to excite." To do that, he proposed one championship day of racing every year, featuring seven different races all run for at least $1 million—purses that would be put up by the breeders. The card, which Gaines called The Parade of Champions, would be held at a different venue every year, in late October or early November, giving horse racing a showdown to rival baseball's World Series and football's Super Bowl. Gaines's proposed Parade of Champions would bring the best horses together every year and revitalize the racing industry.

The concept was received coolly. Many horsemen were skeptical of the idea, while others worried that the event would detract from the spring Triple Crown races. But the racing industry's woes were real, and when an influential group of breeders got behind it, Gaines's idea was put to the test two years later. With its name changed to the Breeders' Cup, the first national thoroughbred championship was hosted by Hollywood Park, California, in 1984. The press and public took note, and 64,254 fans showed up at the park, including such celebrities as Gregory Peck, Elizabeth Taylor, Cary Grant, and Frank Sinatra. The Breeders' Cup, a new Fall Classic, was under way.

At the heart of the Breeders' Cup concept is the need for a balance between the money that can be made by racing thoroughbreds and the money to be made by breeding them. The Breeders' Cup effectively encourages this balance. To become eligible for the Breeders' Cup races, breeders must first nominate stallions by putting up a sum equivalent to one breeding right to the stud. This would range from upwards of $100,000 for the top stallions to considerably less for lesser ones. Once a stallion has been nominated, each of his offspring can be nominated for $500 per foal. By 1988, the Breeders' Cup was able to raise $11 million a year in stallion nominations and $6 million in foal fees. This amount not only covered the $10 million for the purses for the Breeders' Cup program, but also let the Breeders' Cup committee raise purses in various selected stakes races around the country.

Indeed, with so much new purse money available, Gaines's concept of a $1-million-per-race purse was quickly superseded. The seven-race card currently features the $3-million Breeders' Cup Classic, which is run at the Derby distance of a mile and a quarter and serves as the climactic event on the program. The secondary feature is the $2 million Turf, run at a mile and a half. The five other races, all with $1 million purses, are the 1 1/16-mile Juvenile (for two-year-old colts and geldings), the 1 1/16-mile Juvenile Fillies, the 1 1/8-mile Distaff (for fillies and mares three years old and up), the Mile (on the turf), and the six-furlong Sprint. From the outset, the Breeders' Cup has quickly attracted America's most dominant thoroughbreds in every category.

For the first time, owners have been given the incentive to race their star horses longer instead of whisking them off to stud. Consider the case of Alysheba, the 1987 Kentucky Derby and Preakness winner. When he won the $3 million Breeders' Cup Classic as a four-year-old in 1988, he surpassed John Henry to become the all-time leader in earnings. Without the Breeders' Cup program, Alysheba would surely have been retired at the end of his three-year-old season. Although it is always a risk to continue racing a horse, it is the races themselves that bring new fans and new energy into the sport. The Breeders' Cup has made the risk worthwhile.

In fact, the only controversy about the Breeders' Cup has been where it should be held. Gaines's idea of rotating sites has been in effect since 1984, but less than ideal weather conditions in 1985 at New York's Aqueduct and in 1988 at Churchill Downs have led many to urge the establishment of a permanent site at one of the major California or Florida tracks. In addition, with the Breeders' Cup under contract with the NBC television network, a California starting time of eleven A.M. would fit nicely into the network's afternoon, two-to-six-o'clock time slot. Still, many racing people feel it is important to keep the Breeders' Cup moving around the country, and the issue has not been resolved either way. In 1989, the program was held at Florida's Gulfstream Park. Other tracks eager to host the event are the new Arlington International Racecourse near Chicago, the Fair Grounds in New Orleans, Belmont in New York, and Remington Park in Oklahoma.

In the first five years of the Breeders' Cup, trainer D. Wayne Lukas and owner Eugene V. Klein had the most victories in the five programs. But Klein's and Lukas's successes have been partially obscured by the story of trainer Jack Van Berg's quest to win the $3 million Classic.

Van Berg ran in the inaugural Classic at Hollywood Park with Gate Dancer. That year at Hollywood Park, Gate Dancer got hooked up in a torrid, three-way run for the wire with Wild Again and Slew o' Gold. Gate Dancer was moving up on the outside, Wild Again on the rail, Slew o' Gold in the middle. Suddenly, in the last few yards of the race, Wild Again lunged out toward Slew o' Gold, while Gate Dancer moved in on him from the outside. Slew o' Gold faltered, and the very close photo finish revealed that Wild Again had just nudged out Gate Dancer for the win.

The stewards, however, were reviewing the tape. They seemed to be presented with three choices: (a) let the final order of finish stand, (b) take down both Wild Again and second-place Gate Dancer in place of Slew o' Gold, or (c) declare Gate Dancer the winner. In a decision that earned a hearty chorus of boos from the crowd, the stewards took an altogether different option: they left Wild Again the winner, but disqualified Gate Dancer to third while moving Slew o' Gold to second.

Van Berg, of course, was bitterly disappointed. He felt that his horse's erratic running earlier in the year—he had been disqualified from fourth to fifth for interference in the Kentucky Derby—had unfairly influenced the stewards' decision. But Van Berg's career at the Breeders' Cup Classic was only just beginning.

A year later, on a miserable day at Aqueduct Race Track in New York, Van Berg and Gate Dancer were back for another try in the Classic, this time against a field that included such big names as Chief's

Crown, Track Barron, Vanlandingham, and Proud Truth. After letting Vanlandingham and Track Barron set the early pace, Gate Dancer and Proud Truth gradually began to pass horses until they were 1–2 at the stretch call. With Gate Dancer wearing his distinctive, eerie white hood, the two horses fought it out. At the wire, it was Proud Truth on the outside, by a head.

Again Van Berg had come within a few feet of winning the Classic, and again he had failed. In 1986, he sat out the Classic, which was won by the long-shot Skywalker at Santa Anita. In 1987, Van Berg was back, with the Kentucky Derby and Preakness winner, Alysheba.

Alysheba had been stopped short of the Triple Crown by Bet Twice at Belmont. In this Classic, his main competition was to come from Derby winner Ferdinand, who had won at Churchill Downs in 1986 and who was being ridden by fifty-seven-year-old Bill Shoemaker. This was the kind of match that John Gaines might have dreamed of when he came up with the idea for the Breeders' Cup: two Kentucky Derby winners in a race that could never have happened a few years before.

At first, it looked as if neither Ferdinand nor Alysheba would figure in the race as a speedball named Judge Angelucci, named for a Kentucky judge, led all the way to the eighth pole. But grudgingly, the Judge gave way, and Ferdinand made his charge. Ferdinand looked for a moment as if he would be the clear winner, when Alysheba, coming up from as far back as ninth in a twelve-horse field, began a dramatic charge. The two horses hit the wire in tandem. It was only after close inspection of the photo of the finish that the placing judges determined Ferdinand had won by a nose.

At this point, Van Berg had entered three Classics and had lost each $3-million race by a head, a head, and a nose respectively. He came back again in 1988 at Churchill Downs, and this time the gods of horse racing were smiling.

It was a poor day in Louisville. A gloomy darkness was descending, the track was sloppy; from the upper grandstand, fans could barely see what was happening on the track. Van Berg's horse again was Alysheba, who had been even more dominant as a four-year-old than the year before, winning against all kinds of opposition, at all kinds of distances, and under all kinds of track conditions. His day had come at last.

That afternoon Alysheba moved through the gloom like a ghost, taking the lead inside the eighth pole. Seeking the Gold came flying at him on the outside; Alysheba dug in and pulled off to a solid half-length win. Van Berg had won his Classic.

Alysheba's victorious Classic run came 113 years after the first running of the Kentucky Derby. Just as the Derby and the Triple Crown races have done over that time, the Breeders' Cup will produce its legendary horses and unforgettable duels, its own cast of characters, its share of victories and heartbreaks. As of now, the fledgling tradition stands as a testimonial to the racing community's willingness to change—when change, not tradition—is required.

Only two weeks after his triumph in the Classic, Alysheba was officially retired in ceremonies at Churchill Downs. The big horse was taken to the paddock, then galloped down the stretch so the fans could have one last look at him. Then he was put in a van and sent off to the Lane's End Farm near Versailles, Ky., where he would go about the business of imparting his racing essence—his bloodline—to generations of colts and fillies to come.

AT THE END OF THE DAY, long after the crowd has departed and turned the track over to the cleanup crews, it's quiet again on the backstretch. At the winner's barn, the blanket of flowers is apt to be draped over the wall in front of the hero's stall. As darkness gathers, the air is filled with soft laughter and the tinkle of glasses as the trainer, his tie loosened and his coat off, relives the race with the owner, the jockey, and their friends. Finally they are relaxed, the pressure off at least for a while.

Meanwhile, at the barns of the losers, plans are already being made for the next time. A trainer can always find an excuse for a defeat, whether it's a mistake in judgment by the jockey or the condition of the track or a bit of poor racing luck. Maybe just a little adjustment—a new rider or a change in equipment or a different post position—will make the next outcome different. "This is the great thing about racing," trainer D. Wayne Lukas once said. "There's always another race."

Soon the barn area is quiet and virtually deserted. Tomorrow will come soon enough for the horses and the people who work with them. The circus will move on down the road to the next stop on the classic circuit, where yesterday's winner will have to prove himself again and the losers will take another crack, certain in the knowledge that the goddess of fortune will smile kinder the next time. On the racetrack, dreams may be deferred, but they never die.

THE PHOTOGRAPHS

Darby Dan Farm

North Ridge Stallion Complex

Gainesway Stallion Barn

Ocala

Ocala

OVERLEAF *Domino Stud Farm*

Crescent Farm

Donamire Farm

Saratoga

Saratoga

Keeneland outriders

Keeneland Spring Meet

Donamire Training Track

Belmont

Keeneland

"pinched back"

Churchill Downs

Churchill Downs

Spendthrift

Spendthrift

Ocala

Saratoga

Hialeah

Gainesborough Stallion Barn

Hialeah

Keeneland

OVERLEAF *Keeneland Fall Meet*

Preakness at Pimlico

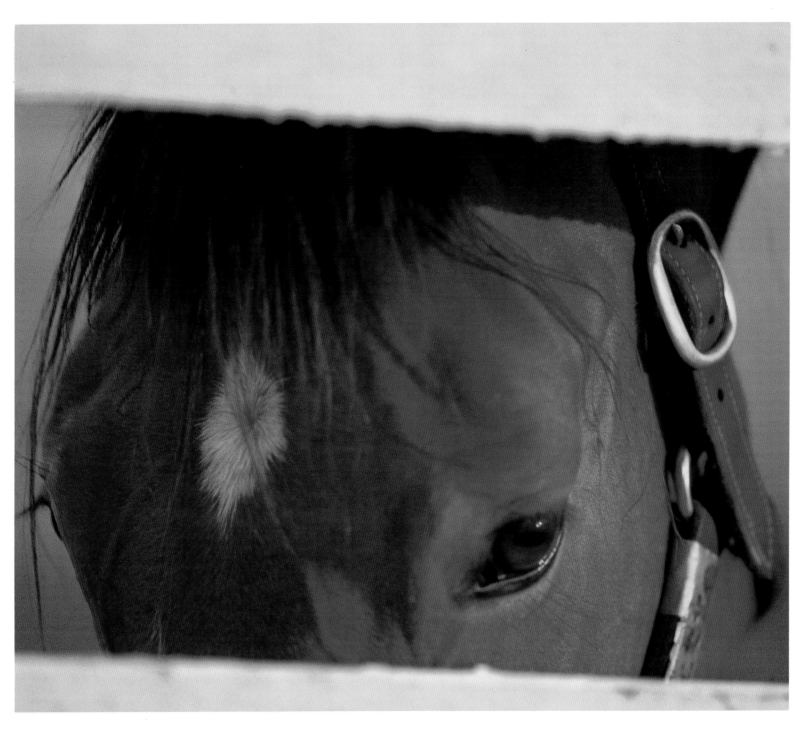

Domino Stud Farm

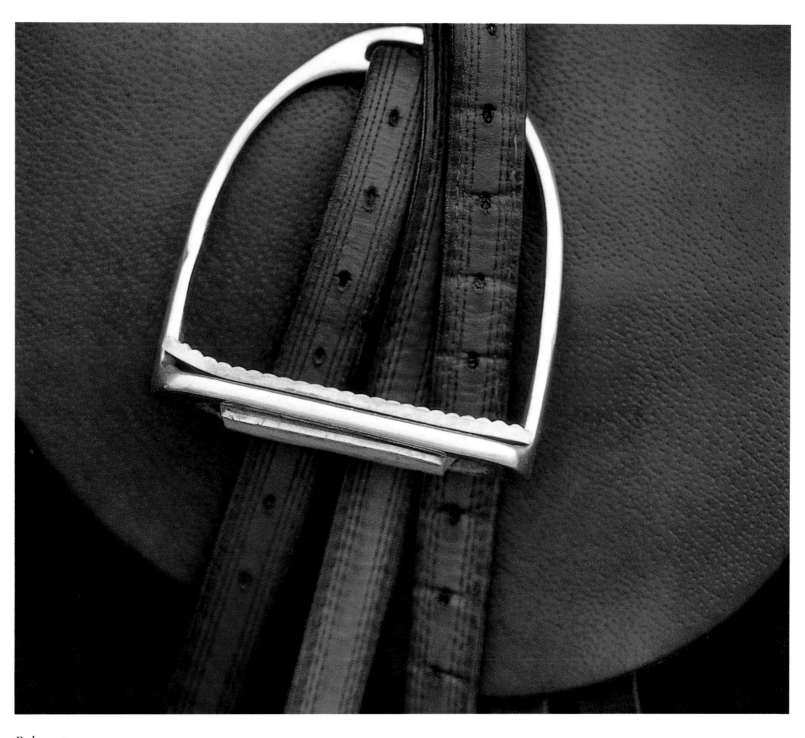

Belmont

Belmont

Gulfstream

Keeneland Spring Meet

Keeneland Spring Meet

OVERLEAF *Out of the Starting Gate*

In the Mud

Keeneland

Darby Dan Farm

Donamire Farm

Stone Farm

Hialeah, going to the morning workout

The Outrider

Keeneland

Churchill Downs

Churchill Downs

Keeneland

Brookside Farm

Breeders' Cup

Jim Beam Day, Turfway Park

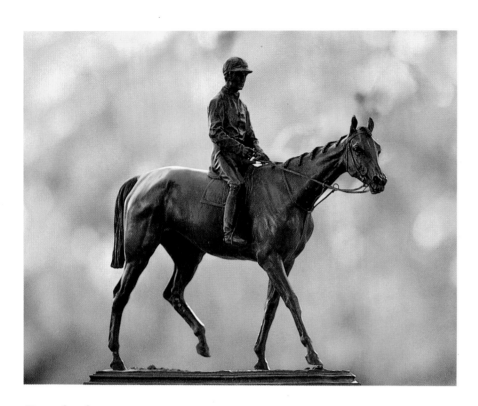

Keeneland

Keeneland

North Ridge Stallion Complex

Turfway Night Racing

Winning Colors's Derby Finish

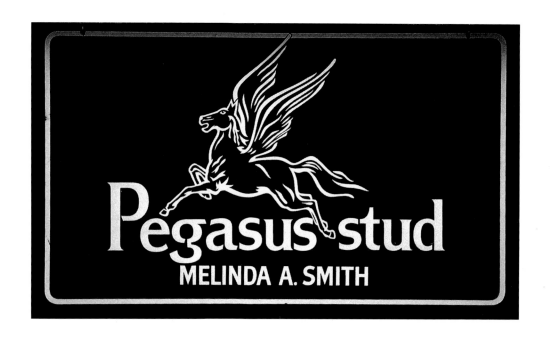

Lanes End Farm

BULL LEA
BROWN
1935   1964
BULL DOG   ROSE L...
BLUE GRASS, WIDENER HANDIC...
... THREE KENTUCKY DERBY ...
ALSO OF WINNERS OF O...
THIRTEEN MILLION DOLLARS...
CITATION
FIRST THOROUGHBRED MILLIONN...
TRIPLE CROWN 1948 $1.08...
BEWITCH
LEADING MONEY WINNING ...
... 1951 — MAY 1962 $46...
ARMED
... MONEY WINNING GELDING
1946 — SEPT. 1962 $817,47...
AND MANY OTHERS
...ING AMERICAN SIRE FIVE ...
...ING BROODMARE SIRE FOUR ...
...EE REPRESENTATIVES IN HALL OF FAME
...RESENTATIVE IN ALL DIVISIONAL TITLES

Calumet Farm

Churchill Downs

Churchill Downs

OVERLEAF *Belmont*

Keeneland

Keeneland, Bucky Salee

Keeneland

Keeneland

Breeders' Cup at Churchill Downs

Churchill Downs

Keeneland

Sales Pavilion at Saratoga

Keeneland Sales

North Ridge Farm

Keeneland

Keeneland Summer Select Sales

Keeneland Summer Select Sales

Crescent Farm

North Ridge Farm

Domino Stud Farm

Domino Stud Farm

Belmont

Keeneland Fall Meet

River Downs

Darby Dan Farm

Buckram Oak Farm

North Ridge Farm

Manchester

Florida Derby at Gulfstream

Hialeah

Overbrook Farm

Gainesway Stallion Complex

OVERLEAF *River Downs*

Taylor Made Farm

Elmendorf

Buckram Oak Farm

Elmendorf

River Downs

Keeneland

Churchill Downs

Gato del Sol, Stone Farm

Keeneland Fall Meet

Buckram Oak Farm

Buckram Oak Farm

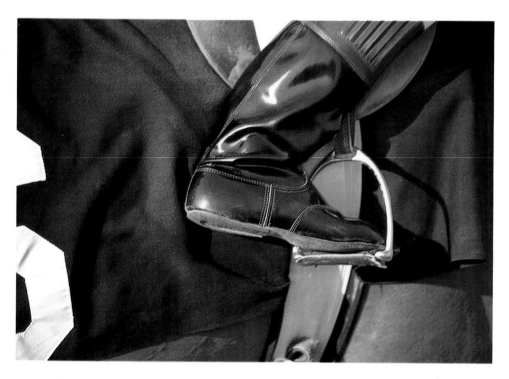

Keeneland

Keeneland

Gainesway Farm

Hamburg Place

OVERLEAF *Manchester Farm*

Dixiana Farm

North Ridge Farm

Spendthrift